IMAGES
of America

BEDFORD AND ITS NEIGHBORS

On the cover: The Bedford Springs Hotel greeted guests from not only across America, but also from around the world. Since 1805, the hotel provided mineral-rich waters to its visitors, a health spa for the mind and body, and an escape for the famous as well as the nameless. If one listens carefully, the music of the brass bands and the echoes of laughter resounding in the Cumberland Valley can still be heard. (Photograph courtesy of Bill Defibaugh.)

IMAGES of America
BEDFORD AND ITS NEIGHBORS

Daniel J. Burns

ARCADIA
PUBLISHING

Copyright © 2005 by Daniel J. Burns
ISBN 978-1-5316-2725-6

Published by Arcadia Publishing
Charleston, South Carolina

Library of Congress Catalog Card Number: 2005935046

For all general information contact Arcadia Publishing at:
Telephone 843-853-2070
Fax 843-853-0044
E-mail sales@arcadiapublishing.com
For customer service and orders:
Toll-Free 1-888-313-2665

Visit us on the Internet at www.arcadiapublishing.com

Contents

Acknowledgments		6
Introduction		7
1.	The Early Days	9
2.	A Community Prospers	15
3.	Old Mother Bedford	27
4.	Bedford's Neighbors	41
5.	A Day in the Life	59
6.	To Learn and Worship	83
7.	Getting Around	95
8.	A Grand Hotel	107

ACKNOWLEDGMENTS

I am a firm believer that things happen for a reason. While looking for a subject for my next book, it was by pure chance that I met the Fort Bedford Museum's curator, Joel Riggle, and after a brief tour of the town, I was hooked by its charm and historical relevance. To Joel and Rachel Riggle, thank you for your hospitality and friendship. There are many others I would like to extend my appreciation to including my friends Steve George, Bill Van Deventer of the Coral Caverns, and Roger Kirwin of Old Bedford Village. I'd like to thank Bill Defibaugh for his generosity in sharing the history of the Bedford Springs Hotel, Dr. Ron Markwood, Oralee Keiffer of the Golden Eagle for her wonderful hospitality, Melissa Jacobs of the Jean Bonnet, Glendon Castille, Gillian Leach and Ruth Mackey of the Pioneer Historical Society, Doug Stuart, Joyce Hercaine of Schellsburg, Gen. Clay Buckingham (retired), Frank Dunkle, and Barb Miller. I am grateful to everyone who generously donated their time, knowledge, and photographs to make this book possible. And again, thanks to my dearest Sarah, you make all of this possible.

I came to Bedford looking for photographs and historical information; what I found were many life-long friends.

INTRODUCTION

In 1751, Robert Ray constructed a log cabin and established a settlement along the Juniata River for the purpose of trading goods, such as pelts and furs, with the Indians. The area became known as Raystown. In 1758, the advance guard of the army of General Forbes built a fort at Raystown during the French and Indian War. Gen. John Stanwix changed the name of the fort to Fort Bedford in honor of the Duke of Bedford, of Bedfordshire, England, and a secretary of state to King George III.

The town, which grew up around and in support of the fort, became a growing community in the mid-1760s, after William Penn was granted a charter of 2,800 acres. The streets and alleys were laid out with four of the streets named after Penn's children: Richard, Juliana, Thomas, and John. Pitt Street, formerly Forbes Road, was named after the British prime minister. Bedford flourished, as it was located along the Forbes Road, which led from Philadelphia to Pittsburgh. The land was rich and fertile and attracted many settlers and farmers.

The population of the area soon expanded, and the need to support those residents increased, making Bedford the regional hub of commerce and industry. As the region grew, however, so did the need to move from point A to point B at a faster pace. The town of Bedford found itself, as many small towns in America have, circumvented by four-lane interstates and a bypass highway. On the positive side, these modern travel conveniences have left the town able to preserve its historic stature, and the entire town is listed as a national historic landmark.

Standing in the town square and gazing about the beautifully restored and preserved buildings, it is easy to imagine a time when gentlemen tipped their hats to passersby, white-gloved ladies carried parasols, and the hooves of carriage horses could be heard on the streets.

One

THE EARLY DAYS

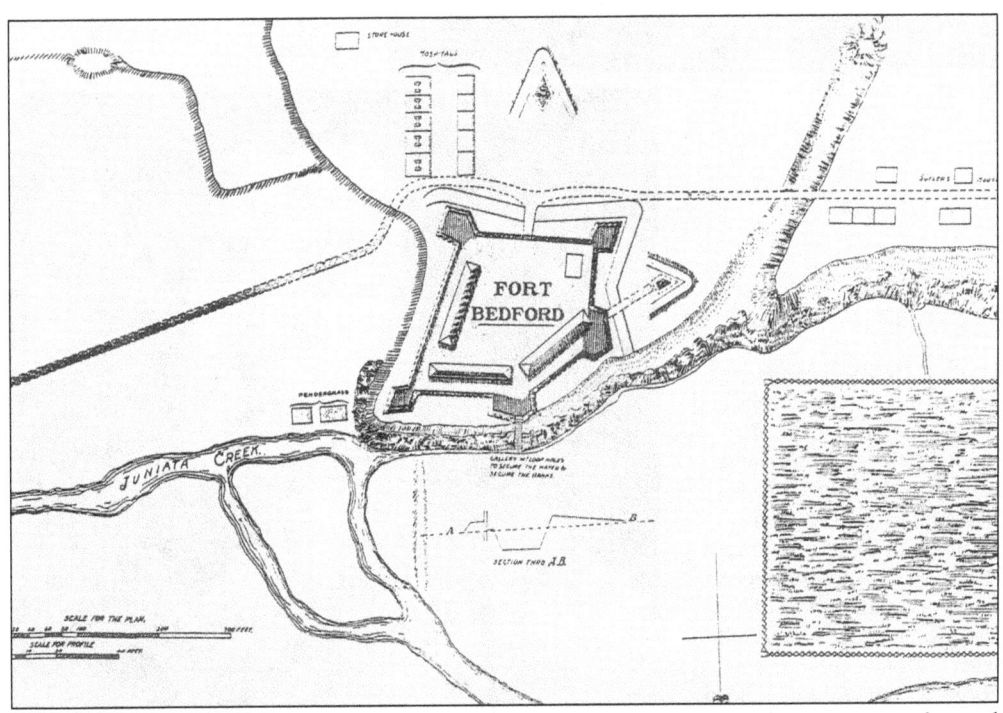

Fort Bedford played a vital role in the French and Indian War, as it served as an outpost for road builders aiding the British drive to capture Fort Duquesne. This map demonstrates the original fort location and shows many features, including the Forbes Road and a v-shaped external defense rampart to the fort's south on the top of the map. The fort was designed to house 5,000 troops and officers, as well as storehouses that held flour, oxen, and sheep.

Gen. John Forbes was commissioned Brigadier General in 1757 and was given command of Her Majesty's forces in America. His orders were to construct a road from Raystown and capture Fort Duquesne. To accomplish this, he amassed an army of 6,000 British and American soldiers. While the road was being constructed, Forbes became gravely ill and later died. Native Americans gave him the name Head of Iron because even though he was gravely ill, his spirit never quit.

Lt. Col. Henry Bouquet was second to General Forbes and took command of the army after Forbes fell ill. A Swiss officer in the English army, Bouquet was an excellent engineer and was recognized as one of the most efficient military commanders of his day. Bouquet is credited with the placement and construction of Fort Bedford. He saw that the land was flat but elevated, with a source of water, as it was at the junction of Dunning's Creek and the Juniata River.

Conestoga wagons carried goods and supplies and were the transportation mode of choice for the settler families and merchants of the 19th century. Depending on the weight of the wagons, they were pulled by teams of two or four horses along narrow paths across the steep mountain road passes. Many of these roads were dubbed "corduroy roads," as they were constructed from the trees that were cut down to make way for the passage.

Bedford was incorporated as a borough in 1795. In 1809, Philadelphia merchant Joshua Gilpin traveled through Bedford to explore business prospects and inspect family land holdings. Gilpin described the view of the area he saw as "beautifully seated on an eminence surrounded by a number of hills handsomely cultivated."

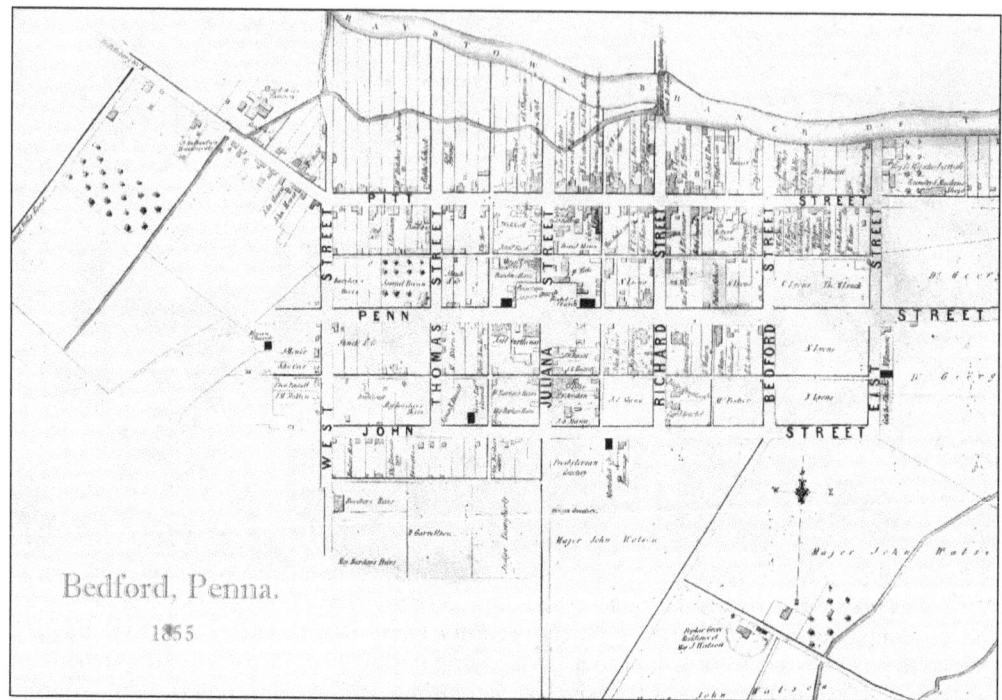

Bedford was known as one of the most substantially built towns in the state of Pennsylvania. Many of the buildings in the business district were constructed of brick or stone. The town boasted a sturdy school building, six churches, two banks, and two newspapers, the *Bedford Inquirer* and the *Bedford Gazette*, which is still published today.

By the turn of the 19th century, Bedford boasted nearly 3,000 residents and over 100 businesses, including a shirt factory, a shirt laundry, about 50 stores, numerous hotels and boarding houses, and 4 meat markets. This photograph, taken in 1896, shows the center of town.

In July 1889, electric lights illuminated the town and surrounding area. A total of 37 arc lights were turned on, with 24 of them set up in the town, 5 on the road to the Bedford Springs, and 8 on the Springs's property. The *Bedford Inquirer* reported, "When the lights were turned on, midnight darkness turned into noonday brilliance."

The area around Bedford is broken by a number of mountain ranges that are a part of the Appalachian system. From east to west, these mountains include Tussey's, Evitt's, Will's, Buffalo, and the Allegheny Mountains. Between these mountains lie magnificent, scenic valleys and rich, fertile soil that produces a yearly variety of fine crops.

This photograph, taken in the late 1860s, depicts a family and their log home, built in 1780. Frontier life in the Bedford area was hard. The winters were harsh, with deep snows and bitter, cold temperatures, and the mountain passes were no less treacherous during the spring rains. In addition to the unforgiving terrain and weather conditions, attacks on settlers by Native Americans continued through the 1780s as a growing number of whites continued to squat on land not legally bought from the Native Americans.

Two

A Community Prospers

On October 19, 1794, Pres. George Washington arrived in Bedford and was the guest of David Espy, Esq., at his house pictured above. Washington summoned the militia to maintain order in the region after it was believed that civil unrest was imminent due to the government's whiskey tax. It was the only time in U.S. history that a sitting president took command of troops in the field. Today, the Espy House is a national landmark that can boast that George Washington really did sleep there.

Built by Dr. John Anderson in the late 1700s, the Anderson mansion was constructed as a rest stop for travelers and merchants. The Golden Eagle Tavern was located on the ground floor of the mansion and served Washington's militia during the Whisky Rebellion. Today, the mansion is the Golden Eagle Inn and continues its rich tradition of serving guests and travelers as a charmingly restored bed-and-breakfast.

The Jean Bonnet Tavern was once known as the Forks Inn because of its position at the junction of two main thoroughfares used by the settlers. The inn, built in 1760, was a much-needed rest stop for those traveling on the Old Forbes Road. The tavern played a key role in local history, including the Whiskey Rebellion of 1794. Today, the Jean Bonnet operates as a restaurant and bed-and-breakfast. Like some of the historic buildings in the area, the two and a half centuries of history are said to live on through strange occurrences and ghostly sightings witnessed by dozens throughout the years.

The Coffee Pot was built as a lunch stand along old Route 30 in 1927. It quickly became a roadside attraction, as only 14 others existed in the country at the time of its construction. The Coffee Pot, saved from demolition, was moved across the street and restored. Visitors may now tour and enjoy this unique piece of Americana.

For decades, the Diebert Mill produced feed, which it sold to the farms in the Bedford area. The mill and its store also contributed to local fashions, as many a little girl attended school clad in a dress that was once a burlap bag that the feed was stored and sold in. At any given time, dressmaking moms could be found in the store looking through the bags, seeking just the right weave.

The Ella Gilchrist Millinery Store opened in the late 1880s. Located in downtown Bedford, the shop served customers as far north as Johnstown and as far south as Cumberland. As the leading milliner in Bedford, local advertisements boasted that Gilchrist's had "silks, ribbons, fancy stamped goods, and fancy neckwear and underwear."

In 1900, there were over 50 stores in and around the downtown Bedford business district. These stores served the surrounding towns of Mann's Choice, Everett, Buffalo Mills, New Baltimore, Osterburg, Schellsburg, New Paris, and Hopewell.

The Chalybeate Springs Hotel was built in 1851 and was originally known as the Funk Springs, after the first owner, George Funk, a local merchant. The hotel was billed as a health resort in the mid-1800s and was visited by many guests seeking the positive health benefits of its mineral springs. The building underwent many alterations over the years. It was a private residence, a tavern, and an apartment complex.

Throughout the 1800s, the town of Bedford was visited by thousands of people seeking the healing powers of the mineral springs that flowed from the surrounding mountains. Although the most noted of these resorts was the Bedford Springs Hotel, it was also out of the financial reach of most of these travelers. The vast majority of visitors to Bedford stayed at other hotels and inns that offered transportation to the spring resorts. One of these is the Grand Central Hotel, pictured here.

Around the beginning of the 20th century, businesses flourished in Bedford. The once small outpost in the wilderness had now grown as a business community, providing goods and services to local residents, as well as the population in the surrounding areas. The town of Bedford had become the premier place to shop.

There were many merchants in Bedford that offered a variety of goods and services including clothing, dry goods, furniture, and variety stores. Shown here is a typical grocery store, which was a one-stop shop for meats, vegetables, baked goods, and confections. One store advertised, "Only the choicest goods stocked."

As well as having a shop in the center of town, the Moorehead Brothers Butchers could be seen traveling Penn, Juliana, and Pitt Streets in their wagon, selling their goods, which included smoked hams, turkeys, and jerked meats.

One of the many great sights along the Lincoln Highway Route 30 corridor is Dunkle's Gulf Station on West Pitt Street. Built in 1933 in art deco fashion, the building is adorned with colorful tile, which is referred to as the Zig Zag Modern style. The station is currently owned and operated by the son of the original owner who is committed to the family tradition of honest work at a fair price.

Simon Oppenheimer was one of the leading men's clothiers in town. His advertising boasted, "No make believes enter into our selling at our store. No make believe that a thing isn't what it isn't. No shams. No false pretenses. Right things called by their right names at the right prices."

In 1900, the place to get the latest news or a copy of *Harper's Weekly* was the Palace Cigar Store, owned by Rudolf G. T. Wolff. The store was well stocked in not only tobaccos, cigars, and all smoking supplies, it also had an inventory of bicycles and various sporting goods. There was a pool parlor on the first floor.

As the town prospered, so did the proprietors that operated the stores and shops in Bedford. Many of the more opulent houses in the area were owned by local merchants, whose names included Calhoun, Wertz, and Diehl.

The S. H. Koontz Music House was located in town and supplied instruments, sheet music, and even uniforms to most of the organized bands in Bedford County. Koontz was known to stock everything from hand-carved wooden drumsticks to piano keys made of the finest imported ivory. Koontz also offered lessons in violin, horn, clarinet, piano, and harp.

As the population grew in and around the town, the need to move goods to and from the surrounding areas increased. Express services, such as this one, filled the need for shipping and transporting items from small bolts of material for dressmaking to large pieces, such as furniture, farming equipment, and manufacturing machinery. Being an expressman required having muscular arms and a strong back.

It can be said that in the early 1700s, most everything west of Philadelphia was considered America's frontier. As explorers traveled through the wilderness via the rugged mountain passes and river valleys, one of the most indispensable tools carried was the Pennsylvania rifle. Early European gunsmiths brought with them the skills and artistry needed to create a weapon that was functional, sturdy, and artistic, with great attention focused on design and detail. Whether it was used for hunting food or fending off an attack, the Pennsylvania rifle was as much a part of America as its creators that settled this land. Pictured here are brothers Milton (left) and David Defibaugh. Along with their father, William, they were skilled craftsmen who made rifles, pistols, clocks, and furniture.

Three
OLD MOTHER BEDFORD

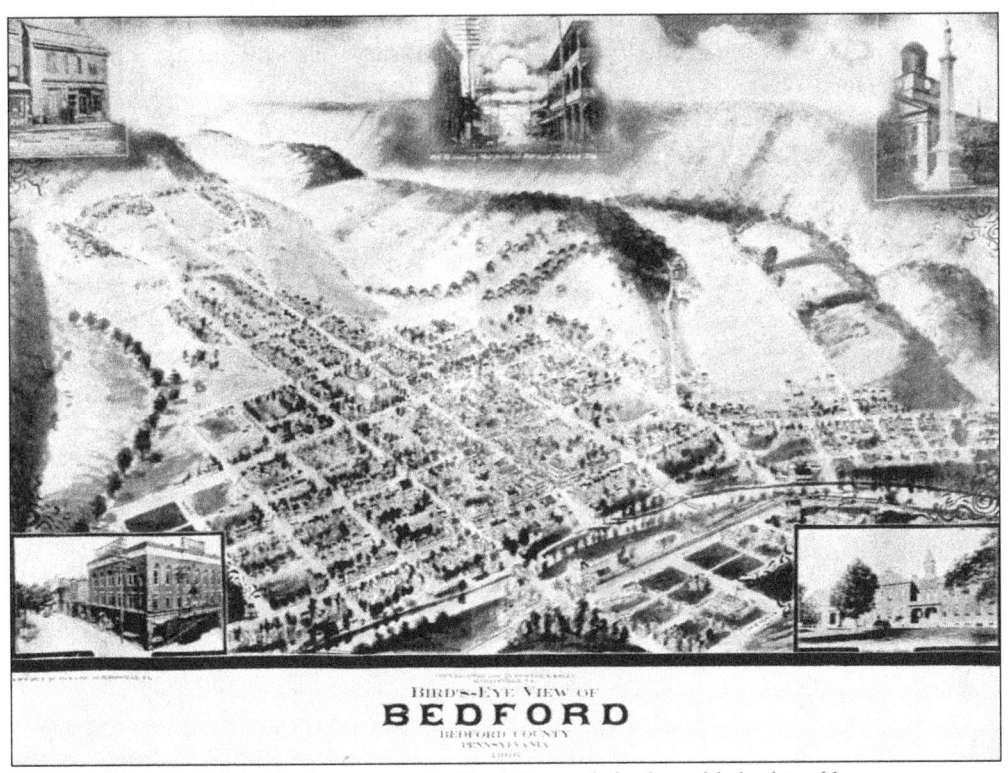

By the beginning of the 20th century, Bedford Borough had established itself as a prosperous community along the Lincoln Highway, formerly known as the Forbes Road. Steady streams of westward travelers made their way through the area along what were the Chambersburg and Bedford Road and the Bedford and Stoystown Turnpike Road. These roadways created the need for the many inns and hotels that were established in and around town. They included the Bedford Inn, the Hotel Waverly, the Fisher House, the Bedford House, and the Grand Central Hotel.

The town of Bedford began primarily as a settlement around Fort Bedford, which played a prominent role in the French and Indian War as well as the Whiskey Rebellion. This etching depicts Bedford's public square in 1850.

Bedford, like many towns in the late 18th and early 19th centuries, had roads and streets that were unpaved. Spring thaws and summer rains brought a muddy mess to area travelers. This picture shows East Pitt Street around 1890.

With the invention of electricity, poles were constructed to carry the wire above the buildings of town. Shown here are the electric poles along West Pitt Street in 1889.

This view of Juliana Street looking toward Pitt Street shows the monument in the distance.

Bedford County was organized from Cumberland County in 1771. The Borough of Bedford's first incorporation was in March 1795. It was not until its second incorporation in 1817 that town officials were elected.

The town square at Pitt and Juliana Streets has always been the popular gathering place for residents to celebrate. No town square would be complete without the gazebo, which provided a venue for the local band and the speechmakers.

Pictured here is one of the many Memorial Day parades that marched down Pitt Street. Bedford residents have always taken much pride in their own who fought for American freedom.

One of the many places that offered accommodations to the weary traveler was the Fort Bedford Inn. Built in 1816, it offered daily and weekly rates, with rooms that had private baths. The inn is now a senior living complex that still proudly displays its magnificent and historic style and architecture.

Still standing today, the Bedford County Jail was built in 1771 and was the location of Bedford's only execution. A local resident and preacher, Cyriacus Spangenberg, was found guilty of murder and hanged after stabbing another man to death. He was hanged in the jail yard in October 1775.

The Bedford County Courthouse was designed and built by architect Solomon Filler in 1828, at a cost of $7,500. In the mid-1870s, an addition was made that contained two large vaults to be used by the recorder of deeds and the county's prothonotary. In the architectural community, the building is known for its unsupported circular stairway. It is the oldest functioning courthouse in the state.

Business in the area flourished as merchants from Everett to Mann's Choice aggressively sold their wares to an expanding population. One advertisement for a general store stated, "All kinds of dry goods are kept in the general store. Fair treatment, just weight, and honorable dealing is my motto."

One of the many fraternal organizations that were established before the 20th century was the Independent Order of Odd Fellows. The Bedford Lodge, built in 1875, shown here, boasted nearly 100 members, who met on Fridays.

There were many floods that affected the Bedford area, including the flood of September 1896, shown here. Others included the Pumpkin Flood in 1810, the flood of 1847, which washed away many local bridges, and the Johnstown flood of 1889. On June 7, 1889, the *Bedford Gazette* reported an account of the Johnstown flood as "A Black Pall of Woe." The Gazette described, "No storm ever did so much damage to Bedford County. Barns, bridges, saw-mills, gristmills, and houses were swept away." Locally, those in Everett suffered the greatest damage, with many losing buildings and livestock. It was believed that over 200 Bedford residents were living in Johnstown at the time of the disaster, and within hours of the flood, wagons full of food and supplies were on their way to those affected, as the people of Bedford reached out to help their neighbors to the north.

The mountains around Bedford are known as a hunter's paradise, as the region has always had a large population of white tail deer and turkey. Pictured here is a hunting party at a lodge in 1901.

To keep foods cold at home, many residents solicited the services of the iceman. The Wilson Lysinger Ice House promoted business by advertising, "Manufactured by Dame Nature, sold and delivered in large or small quantities."

The Bedford Borough Historic District boasts architectural styles as varied as the settlers who made this celebrated community their home over two centuries ago. The many styles represented include Colonial, Victorian, art deco, Greek Revival, bungaloid, Second Renaissance Revival, Federal, Italianate, Georgian, beaux arts, and Second Empire. The buildings were constructed utilizing many materials including log and frame with shiplap, clapboard, brick, and stone. It is interesting to note that none of the varied styles are clustered in one area. All are intermingled throughout the community. The post office, pictured here, was constructed of Indian limestone in 1915 in the neoclassical style.

Known as the "Old Man" on the monument, the granite Civil War soldier stands looking east toward the battlefields of Gettysburg. Erected in 1890, in the middle of the intersection of Penn and Juliana Streets, the 30-ton monument was moved in 1957 to the corner of the town square. The Old Man was positioned so he may still look to the east in honor of those who fought to "perpetuate the government."

Prior to the establishment of the local fire department, many house fires were fought by the residents and neighbors close enough to help. Too often, buildings were destroyed when stray fireplace embers or candles ignited dry wooden structures, as pictured here.

Pictured above, the Bedford Museum is located near the site of the original British Fort Bedford, built in 1758, one of many built along the Forbes Road, which led to the confluence of the Monongahela and Ohio Rivers. The fort was constructed because of its strategic location at the intersection of both east-west and north-south routes. Fort Bedford was the rendezvous for over 7,000 British troops under the leadership of General Bouquet. It was these troops that defeated the French at Fort Duquesne in modern-day Pittsburgh. In 1958, the museum was rededicated in a ceremony attended by many dignitaries, including the Duke of Bedford, England, as well as representatives from state and local government. It stands today as a museum extoling the history of Bedford.

Located on a site that was once a prehistoric settlement dating as far back as 3000 BC and was a Monongahela Indian village in AD 1500, Old Bedford Village is comprised of buildings that were chosen for their historical significance in and around Bedford County. These structures were dismantled, brought to this site, and reassembled in an effort to preserve the architecture and artifacts of Colonial American life. The village was opened to the public on July 4, 1976, and exists today as a living history museum. Visitors can stroll along the village's streets and find themselves back in time, enjoying the craftsmen, artisans, displays, and demonstrations of the American frontier.

Four
BEDFORD'S NEIGHBORS

Located just a few miles west of Bedford is the town of Mann's Choice. In 1848, Congressman Job Mann was tasked with naming a village that was selected as a location for a new post office in Harrison Township. Before the congressman named the location, postal maps were printed with the label "Mann's Choice." The name was never changed. Pictured here is the Coral Caverns, originally opened as the Wonderland Cavern in 1932. The cavern has the only fossilized coral reef in the world that is open to the public. The Coral Caverns, a popular tourist destination, also boasts the largest collection of marine fossils, including prehistoric animals and petrified woods.

Many businesses flourished in Mann's Choice, including the A. H. and W. H. Faule Store, pictured here.

C. L. Hollers was a popular stop for travelers who were en route between Bedford and Cumberland.

The White Sulphur Springs Hotel, located on Will's Mountain in Mann's Choice, is a private retreat for military personnel and their families. The hotel began as a tavern, as stated in records dating back to 1771. The hotel, as seen here, was built in 1884, and accommodated travelers on Will's Mountain and Mulligan's Cove. The buildings remain well maintained, with their simplistic beauty matched only by the surrounding old-growth forest, one of the few still remaining in Pennsylvania.

At the intersection of Routes 30 and 96, a few miles due west of Bedford, is the historic town of Schellsburg. In 1799, John Schell and his family settled along the banks of the Shawnee Cabin Creek in an area originally known as Nine Mile Tract.

In 1801, Schell bought the deed to land at the foot of the Allegheny Mountains. By the spring of 1809, with the construction of homes, stores, and a blacksmith shop, Schellsburg was born and the town began to flourish.

One of the many traditions brought by German immigrants was the holiday celebration of belsnickling. At Christmas time, belsnicklers would travel in groups from farm to farm after dusk, often being boisterous and making merry. They were clad in costumes that would hide all features, including their faces and genders. Although they were not wanted at all of the houses they visited, when welcomed, they were invited in and given refreshments. These snacks were likely to be cookies and cider and were offered only after they revealed themselves. Pictured here are some Schellsburg belsnicklers.

Pictured here, the residents of Schellsburg celebrate the town's Centennial in grand fashion. The parade featured marching schoolchildren, bands, and veterans of the Civil War.

The town of Everett, originally called Bloody Run, was renamed after the well-known orator Edward Everett, best remembered for accompanying Pres. Abraham Lincoln at the Gettysburg Address.

Pictured here is the Union Hotel on East Main Street. Originally on this site stood a stone structure that was used as a store and residence for Michael Barndollar, a leading citizen.

As part of the Lincoln Highway Heritage Corridor, Everett boasts a historical significance for its varied architecture and its location on the Forbes Road. Many industrial innovations were first seen in Everett, including the first portable sawmill in 1868.

Located on present-day Route 30, between Bedford and Everett, is the Defibaugh Tavern. The tavern was built around 1784 by Casper Defibaugh, who immigrated to America from Germany in the 1750s. Also known as the Willows, it is historically significant because it is believed to have been used as a meeting place for local farmers during the Whiskey Rebellion. Although there are no official records indicating that the Defibaughs were involved in the insurrection or that the tavern was a meeting place for those who rebelled, well-known family feelings about the whiskey tax indicate that it is likely that the tavern was close to the center of the controversy.

Built between 1813 and 1819, the Juniata Crossings Lodge is located east of Everett on Route 30. The lodge was originally constructed as a stagecoach stop for travelers. The inn's first liquor license was issued in 1809.

One of the many companies that maintained the road and oversaw the transportation of passengers in that time was the Philadelphia and Lancaster Company. Such businesses were known as turnpike companies and helped make inns like the Juniata Crossings Lodge popular.

The inn stands as a three-story building that was constructed of stone and native timber. Its nine guestrooms, four with fireplaces, surely gave comfort to many weary travelers on the Chambersburg-Bedford Turnpike.

When the inn opened its doors in 1818, the third floor was primarily used for storage, but it was rumored that there was a crawlspace that was utilized by the Underground Railroad. The Juniata Crossings Lodge has been preserved and stands today as a country store, complete with all of its original charm.

At the beginning of the 19th century, Bedford saw a new age of prosperity as agriculture and commerce combined. Industry also began to flourish in the area as Bedford began to expand the transportation of coal and timber.

The town of Hyndman's first settler was a man named Samuel Waters who lived in nearby Wills Creek. Around 1800, two men, Amos Raley and Jacob Burkett, began a boat building business, as water transportation was needed to move grain to Cumberland, Maryland.

Hyndman was named after the Baltimore and Ohio Railroad's superintendent, E. K. Hyndman. The town was incorporated in 1877, with the primary industry being brick manufacturing.

Like many of the communities in Bedford County, Hyndman contributed to the commercial and cultural growth of the region by establishing its own industry and infrastructure.

The Columbia Bridge Works of Dayton, Ohio, was one of many companies that helped connect the many communities and small towns in the Bedford area. Pictured here is the Schellsburg Street Bridge in Hyndman.

Pictured here is one of the many historic attractions around the Bedford area. The Revolutionary War Shot Factory is located less that a mile south of the Ship Hotel, located on Route 30. Today, the building is in private use.

In many towns in early, rural America, the streets were wide and consisted of dirt. This made for a sufficient surface because they were mainly traversed by horses, but during the spring rains, these thoroughfares quickly became muddy bogs.

Among the many industries in Bedford during the 1920s, the area boasted the only peanut factory in the United States, pictured here.

When the first explorers entered the Cumberland Valley and Bedford area in the early 1700s, they saw the tall, magnificent mountains; lush, green valleys; and clear, spring-fed streams. A visitor today can easily see that when it comes to the vistas, little has changed in 300 years.

In the 1790s, the area now known as Rainsburg was settled by James Donahoe. Donahoe and several other businessmen, including Samuel Cessna and John Gump, had established a community, and by 1856, that community had become the borough of Rainsburg.

Sam Gump was originally a Maryland resident who moved to Bedford County. Upon arriving in Rainsburg, Gump opened a carpentry business and soon became the town's justice of the peace, a trusted position.

In 1884, Samuel Williams moved his family to Rainsburg, where he later founded the Allegheny Male and Female Seminary. The school enjoyed only a brief success until the start of the Civil War. Many of the students left the school to fight for their cause.

The town of Saxton was incorporated as a borough in 1866, complete with a post office, shown here. Saxton may be better known as the site of the massacre of Capt. William Phillips's Rangers in 1770.

One of the most famous landmarks in the Bedford area was the Ship Hotel on the old Lincoln Highway, Route 30. Originally constructed to resemble a castle courtyard, it was remodeled in 1932 to look like a steam ship, complete with dining facilities, hotel rooms, and observation decks. Tourists came from all over to see the "three-state and seven-county" view from high in the Allegheny Mountains. Some of the more famous visitors to the ship included Will Rogers, Thomas Edison, Henry Ford, and Calvin Coolidge. The hotel fell into disrepair before it was destroyed by fire in 2001.

Just north of Bedford is the town of Osterburg. Pictured here in 1915, the Osterburg Band was the only band in the county to be chartered. The town was founded by John Oster, who migrated north from Hagarstown, Maryland, in the mid-1780s.

From the time the first settlements were established in the wilderness, the residents of Bedford always took pride in their community. No matter what the challenge, they worked the land to raise their families and never failed to help a neighbor in need. It is no surprise that the character and fortitude that was needed to forge this country can still be found in Bedford.

Five

A Day in the Life

Formerly a part of Cumberland County, Bedford County was established in 1771. During that time, the county made up most of the southern part of the state, an area of over 9,000 square miles. Several counties have been formed from parts of Bedford County, including Westmoreland, Somerset, Blair, Cambria, and Fulton. This is how the term Old Mother Bedford came to be. As this area of Pennsylvania grew, so did the population, as generations of settlers made this region their home and raised their families.

A young lady sits at a desk and, with quill in hand, writes a letter. She is unaware that this is soon to be an art all but lost to telephones, text messages, and e-mail.

In this 1896 photograph, it is obvious that the condition of a young man's room has seen few changes in 100 years.

During the mid- to late 1800s, there were 30 members of the Bedford County Bar. These attorneys included William Schell, Humphrey Tate, F. E. Colvin, Harry Cessna, and Howard Cessna. Regular court in Bedford was held in the first two weeks of February, April, September, and November. The first week was for criminal cases, and the second was for civil.

One of the many historic buildings in Bedford is the Barclay House on Juliana Street. The house was built for John Jacob Barclay in 1889. He served as a Union lieutenant in the Civil War and was imprisoned in Virginia after being wounded. The Barclays were a very prominent family in the late 1800s.

In 1900, a local newspaper reported that Bedford's present railroad facilities were limited to the Bedford Division of the Pennsylvania Railroad, which made good connections, however, the main line was slow because it conducted a heavy trade.

Courting in Bedford was not much different from anywhere else in the late 19th century. A typical date usually consisted of a visit on the porch swing on a star-filled evening or a Sunday afternoon stroll through the countryside.

In August 1817, the first water reservoir was constructed at a cost of $2,000. It had a 16,000-gallon capacity and supplied water to the residents of Bedford the following winter.

Many of the roads and trails through the area, which are some of the oldest in Pennsylvania, followed the original paths used by the Native Americans. In the early days, going could be tough and very bumpy, as road surfaces were made of wood, gravel, and large stones.

In 1900, there were seven secret organizations in the Bedford area. They included the Independent Order of Odd Fellows, the Knights of the Golden Eagle, the Patrons of Husbandry, the Grand Army of the Republic, the Knights of Pythias, the Patriotic Order Sons of America, and the Free and Accepted Masons.

In the early 1900s, the grocery stores around the Bedford area advertised specials in the local newspapers. Some of the sales included four cans of sweet corn for 27¢, 24 pounds of Pillsbury's Best Flour for 77¢, and two pounds of coffee for 49¢.

Many of the schools in the 19th century were geared specifically toward specialized education. One such school boasted, "Advanced studies that prepare young men and women for the teaching business. Handsome buildings, a strong teaching force ensure the best results for our students."

The recollections of people who grew up in Bedford are filled with stories of wonderful childhoods. Whether it is was playing with friends on a warm day or dressing in Sunday best, a day in the life was always a good day.

Population trends in Bedford were slow compared to those statewide. In 1790, the population of Bedford County was a little over 13,000, while Pennsylvania had nearly 435,000 residents. In 1990, Bedford's population was 48,000, while the state had a total population of nearly 12 million.

Stella Mann, the author of the following poem, was born and educated in Bedford but moved away briefly. Upon her return she wrote, "Dear Bedford, we all know you're accused of being slow. But we love you all the same with every letter of your name. When our last day comes along, Dyin' in some other town? Oh, no so peaceful still, rest us on old Bedford's hill."

In 1834, the official measured distance between Pittsburgh and Philadelphia was 303 miles. Traveling by stagecoach took three days, including stops to rest and water the horses, and the fare cost between $10 and $22, depending on the line used.

In 1897, it was written of the *Bedford Gazette*: "As a newspaper, it deserves all good things that can come to it. The Gazette is one of the handsomest of Pennsylvania's county newspapers. If it isn't in the Gazette, it didn't happen."

After the French and Indian War, it was realized that many of the foreign mercenaries, who were mostly European, were absorbed into the local communities. A popular new vocation for some of these unscrupulous men was to find a flock of the religious needy and pose as ministers. These men would preside over baptisms, burial rights, and even weddings.

It may be surprising for some to know that many Bedford residents can trace their lineage in Pennsylvania as far back as the 1600s and extending over seven generations.

With the expansion of rail transportation and the improvements of the road system in the area, families who were once far from each other could now be reunited more easily, with less time devoted to travel.

In the 1890s, Bedford was a very popular destination for daily and extended excursions. The train fare from Pittsburgh was about $7 one-way, but provided an escape from the Smoky City.

It may be hard to imagine a time without television, malls, and multiplex movie theatres, but in the late 19th century, one of the best forms of entertainment was a picnic outing with the family in the countryside or along the banks of the Juniata River.

Competition for the monies made by the area's farmers and merchants was fierce as banks vied for local business. They included the J. G. Hartley and Company Bank of Bedford, the First National Bank of Bedford, the Everett Bank of Everett, and the National Bank of South Pennsylvania in Hyndman.

The story of the lost children of the Alleghenies began on April 24, 1856, when two children, Joseph Cox, age five, and his older brother George, age seven, wandered away from their parents' cabin at the base of the Allegheny Mountains. By early afternoon that day, 200 searchers were in the woods seeking the children. By the next day, there were over 1,000 searchers on the mountain, but by nightfall the only evidence found was a few footprints in the soil. A local man named Jacob Dibert claimed to have a dream that showed him where the children were located. After more than a week had passed, searchers followed the visions from Dibert's dream and found the children deceased on the mountain. Pictured here is the monument that is dedicated to those children.

During the Victorian days, Bedford had a reputation for being a quiet community, as one writer phrased it, "free from the scallywags that infest cities like Philadelphia and Baltimore." Crime was very low here and the people felt safe.

By 1900, Bedford had become known for its excellent school system, and some families moved to the area just so their children could have a Bedford education.

In the mid-19th century, the list of occupations was short, with most of them being that of labor. These occupations included farmer, miller, weaver, merchant, well digger, innkeeper, brick maker, stonemason, distiller, and cabinetmaker. The term gentleman was also used and referred to one who was either affluent or retired.

The first chief burgess, elected in Bedford on February 5, 1817, was James Russell, a well-known attorney at the time. After his election, Russell hired architect Solomon Filler to build him a house, which now stands on South Juliana Street.

The Bedford County Fair, which began in 1852, remains to this day the most anticipated event in town. Initiated by the Bedford County Agricultural Society, the fair has continued the tradition of animal exhibitions, farm shows, and contests that feature local fare.

The town of Bedford has a proud heritage of residents who have been eager to serve in the military. From the Revolution to modern-day conflicts, the men and women of Bedford have answered the call to serve our country. Pictured here are the men of Company L of the 8th Pennsylvania Infantry. This photograph was taken August 6, 1917.

In the 19th century, having a photograph taken was a very expensive proposition. Owning the equipment was far beyond the economic reach of most families, making the town photographer a valuable and much-in-demand member of the community. W. A. Morehouse, Bedford's master photographer, advertised his services by stating, "Wilbur A. Morehouse, all the people say, in finishing pictures does work that will stay. Ladies who want to look pretty and nice, by coming to Morehouse are sure to come twice. Under no circumstances will your work be slight, Retouching all faces until they're made right."

In 1894, the author of a book on how important it is for a man to find the right mate wrote, "Marry a young lady who is known for her manners, good taste, and good general attributes. A sensible girl sees life as it is. Beware of music hall girls or ones who are fast."

An advertisement in a local newspaper read, "Does your back ache? Do you have pains across your kidneys? Is your complexion chalky, gray, or white? If so, don't hesitate for a moment. See your druggist for Swamp Root! The results will surprise you."

The Pennsylvania tax rolls of 1796 listed a population of a little over 1,000, with 132 dwellings and 96 barns. Most of these buildings were constructed of logs, a few of cut board, and a couple of stone.

Before the 20th century, Bedford hosted many visitors who came to the country to enjoy the clean air. The hotels and inns that accommodated them included the Bedford Springs, Bedford House, Hotel Arlington, Union House, and the Washington House. These, as well as other hotels in the area, made available over 1,500 guest rooms within a five-mile radius.

Vaughn Whisker, a local historian and writer, described the first settlers of the Bedford area as, "the cornerstone and foundation of present and future generations. They came here carrying bibles, an ax, a rifle, and a high determination to live, work, and die on their lands."

In the 18th and 19th centuries, life in Bedford was hard for most. The man of the house, as well as his sons, had to be a jack-of-all-trades. In many cases, one had to have good farming skills and be a fairly skilled carpenter and blacksmith. Some were lucky enough to be able to hire others to perform skilled labor.

Another historically significant structure in Bedford was the Bedford County Alms House. Constructed in 1873, the Alms House was built for the poor of the area and provided food and shelter to people who otherwise may not have survived. Houses like the Bedford Alms were not free, as residents had to work for their room and board.

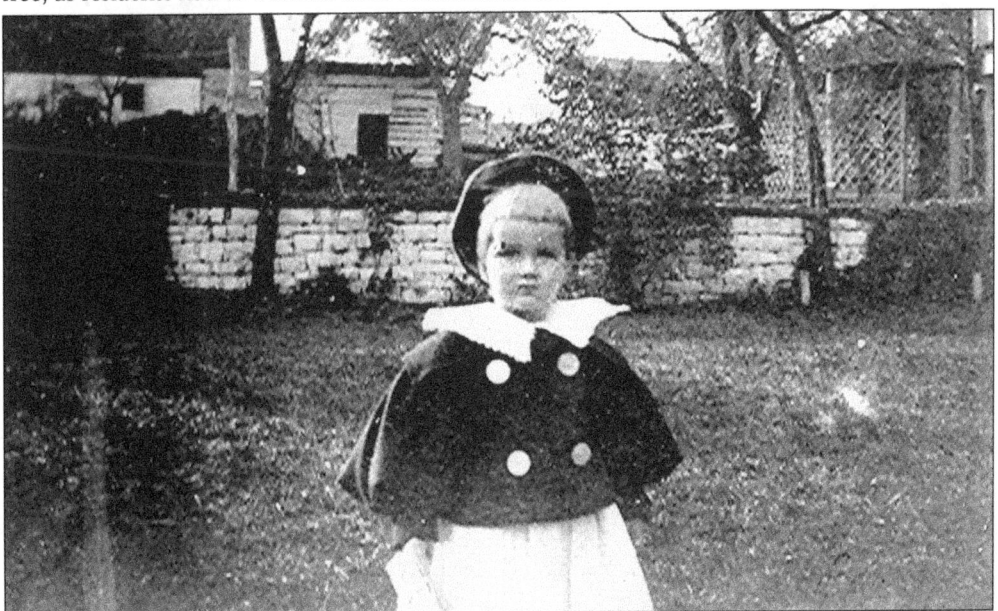

Places like the Bedford Alms House were not uncommon in the area. Many such institutions gave shelter to the mentally ill, the deaf, the handicapped, the homeless, and the destitute. Although the cause was a noble one, the names of the residents were often published in the local newspapers.

Over the years, there have been many famous visitors to the Bedford area. During the 19th century, those visitors included John Brown of Harper's Ferry, Daniel Webster, Thaddeus Stevens, General "Mad Anthony" Wayne, and Cornstalk, chief of the Shawnee Indians.

By the mid-1850s, most of the area schools recognized not only the need for a sound mind but a sound body as well. Secondary schools and schools of higher education offered athletic programs, some even promoting competition between each institution.

Margaret Frazier was a proprietress of a tavern on Pitt Street. Her son, William, born in 1759, was the first recorded white child born in Bedford. Pictured here is the only known sketch of William in his later years.

One of the favorite events in any community is still the Main Street parade. Pictured here is the Armistice Day Parade of 1919, complete with marching bands and returning soldiers.

Like it was many years ago, Bedford is proud of its heritage and history, as the many streets, buildings, and attractions demonstrate. Standing in the center and looking around the town square is like stepping back in time.

One early writer gave the following description of Bedford and the surrounding area, "Owing to the elevated position of the town and its being surrounded by mountains, the location is most beautiful and the air invigorating. The scenery in and about the town is extensive, varied, and beautiful."

Six
TO LEARN AND WORSHIP

The Pennsylvania Constitution of 1790 sanctioned the organization of schools in the Commonwealth for the education of all children, rich and poor. This was known as the Pauper School Law. In 1834, a state law known as the Free School Act was enacted to provide free education in the public schools to the children of Pennsylvania, only now with the assistance of state funds. Many schools resisted this act, and it was not until 1848 that schools were mandated by law to abide by state requirements.

Many of the early schools were one-room schoolhouses that had classes sometimes only four months out of the year, depending on the weather.

Student populations ranged in age from 5 to 25. Most of the teachers were men hired by individual towns and communities that built and maintained their area's school. Discipline was often harsh, but the day's lesson started with a prayer.

Pictured here is the Eight-Square School. Originally located in East St. Clair Township, it was relocated to Old Bedford Village in 1975. The school was built in 1851 and could seat 70 students. It was an active school until it closed in 1932.

Before the construction of newer and more modern schools that had central heating, it was the responsibility of the boys in the class to bring firewood for the pot-bellied stove that warmed the room.

In early days of structured education, when school was not in for students, the schoolmasters themselves were in school for more instruction, as most of them had nothing more than an elementary education.

Most schools divided the students into two groups. The first, or primary, level, consisting of grades one through four, studied basic English and math. The second level, consisting of grades five through eight, studied writing and spelling.

In the early 1800s, education primarily stopped after the elementary level, unless a pupil was lucky enough to have the funds for a private education. It was not until the mid-1800s that high schools were established in the region.

Prior to the establishment of a countywide school system, many children were taught in their homes by private tutors. Most of these tutors were highly educated teachers who specialized in specific subjects, such as grammar and mathematics.

Contrary to popular belief, most students who attended these rural schools did not have to travel uphill both ways, nearly all wore shoes, and in the event of a large snowfall, the school was likely to be closed.

Fortunately for the students, school was not all work. Students, much like today, were given recess and recreation breaks during the school day. Some of the games included Red Rover, tag, and kick ball.

St. Thomas the Apostle Catholic Church was founded by the "Prince Priest of the Alleghenies," Fr. Demetrius Gallitzin, in 1816. The original church was constructed in 1817 and still stands next to the original cemetery. A growing population necessitated the construction of a larger building, which was erected in 1868. In October 1958, the original church was declared a community shrine and restored in its present location. St. Thomas the Apostle has been called an artistic jewel, as the alter is adorned with statues hand-carved in Europe.

Built in 1879, the St. James Episcopal Church is located on South Richard Street. The church is an exact replica of one in London, England, designed and built by Christopher Wren.

Trinity Lutheran Church, shown here, was constructed on the Bedford town square. This building was not the congregation's first, as the Lutherans and the Reformed Church together had previously occupied a log structure in the late 1700s. The existing church was built after the two congregations separated in 1849.

The Presbyterian church, shown here, was built in 1829 and is the third oldest church in Bedford County. Initially, Presbyterians held services in the old courthouse on the town's square. In 1810, a small brick building was erected on the lot where the present-day church stands.

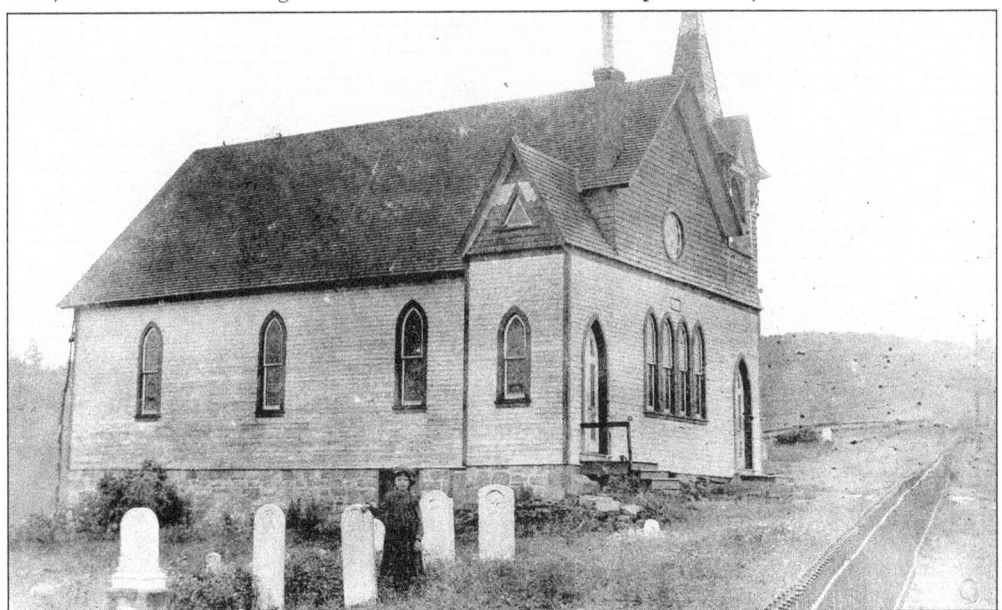

Pictured here is the Trinity Reformed Church in Mann's Choice. Other churches in the area include the Presbyterian church, Bedford Bible Church, Bedford United Methodist Church, Bedford Valley Assembly of God, Calvary Baptist, Dunning's Creek Church of the Brethren, and the Church of the Nazerene.

At the beginning of the 20th century, there were 62 places of worship in the Bedford area. They included 15 Methodist, 11 Lutheran, 6 Christian, 11 Reformed, 5 Presbyterian, 3 Evangelical, a Catholic, and a Baptist.

One of the two schools that provided a higher education in Bedford County in the mid-19th century was the Allegheny Male and Female Seminary in Rainsburg. Its doors opened in 1853, and the cost of an education included $3 for English classes and $4 to $8 for different levels of art classes. Piano lessons started at $10.

The Old Log Church, located in Schellsburg, was built on land donated by John Schell in 1807. The church was constructed to accommodate the combined followers of Lutheran and Reformed congregations. Although a stove was purchased and put into service in 1809, the worshipers, who sat on logs, often brought their dogs to help keep their feet warm.

The Schellsburg Cemetery surrounds the Old Log Church. The cemetery hosts the graves of the Schell family and most of its descendants. In 2002, the Old Log Church and Cemetery Preservation Society was formed for the purpose of preserving the church and cemetery for future generations.

Shown here is a popular architectural feature found in many early Colonial churches. The wineglass pulpit elevated preachers so that the flock may see and hear the sermons of its religious leaders.

One of the many religious organizations that did good works in the community was the Douglas Dorcas Society, whose charge it was to administer relief to the poor. Pictured here is the local chapter at the Osterburg Parsonage.

Seven
Getting Around

Getting around in the Bedford area could often be a substantial challenge. Travelers were confronted with a variety of adverse conditions, ranging from inclement weather to attacks by Native Americans. It is known that Dr. John Anderson, the founder of the Bedford Springs Hotel, carried a pistol when riding the local paths and trails. Most early roads were merely paths, usually only wide enough for one cart to pass, thus making a wagon traveling in the opposite direction yield by pulling to the side. This maneuver was made additionally treacherous by wet or muddy road conditions.

Horses were the most prized and protected animals on the Colonial frontier. Used not only for transportation, most families depended on the horses for their farming chores. It was estimated that at the beginning of the 19th century, there were over 77,000 owned horses in Bedford County.

Carriages were utilized for the transportation of people and goods throughout the area. Along the Forbes Road, inns were established approximately every 10 miles, not for the comfort of the traveler, but to rest the horses.

Named "Tally Ho's," these carriages were employed to transport visitors to the area attractions from the local hotels. It is believed that these transports were given their name by the owners of the Defibaugh Tavern, east of Bedford.

Pictured here is a young lad employed by the Bedford Springs Hotel. His duties included running errands for staff members and guests and often transporting people around the hotel. These drivers were called hacks.

Those individuals who were of good health and vigor were often seen riding bicycles in Bedford. Viewed then as more of a necessity than a sport, bicycle riding was very common, with many general stores selling all of the parts and accessories.

With the introduction of steam-powered tractors in the 1870s, farming became easier for the farmer and less burdensome for the horse. Pictured here is a bark train from around 1900.

Many of these steam-powered tractors were used for transporting crops from the field to the market. Steam engines were capable of pulling larger and heavier loads than horses and did not tire.

The Narrows Bridge, shown here along Route 30 west of Bedford near Everett, was dedicated the same day as the Ship Hotel in 1933. It was constructed to replace an iron truss bridge to better accommodate increased traffic.

Shown here is the Juniata Crossings Bridge. Spanning the Raystown branch of the Juniata River, this two-lane covered bridge was washed away during the 1936 flood.

The railroad depot in Bedford was always a hub of activity, as trains to and from Pittsburgh, Cumberland, and Altoona arrived and departed daily with goods and passengers.

In 1904, a young mechanical genius named Chester Karns from Everett built a horseless carriage, known as the Karn's Kar. Young Karns had high hopes of mass-producing the machine but failed to secure the financial backing needed to make his dream a reality. A man named Henry Ford from Detroit had the same vision and was able to secure the monies needed to make his a reality. Chester Karns was a life-long resident and even one-time mayor of Everett. He died in 1979.

For settlers making a new life in the western region of Pennsylvania, the seemingly lowest passage through the Allegheny Mountains was through Bedford. Establishing one of the first toll road systems in America gave the town the opportunity to collect revenues from those making passage.

The toll costs included 6¢ for every 20 sheep and 12¢ for every 20 cattle. A sled or sleigh was 2¢, but a four-wheeled cart drawn by 4 horses had to pay 20¢. Exemptions to toll-paying included attending church or funerals and militiamen on days of training.

This photograph, taken in 1919, shows the motortruck train, which traveled from the nation's capital to San Francisco via the Lincoln Highway. The project was the brainchild of Dr. S. M. Johnson, who felt that that there should be a designated starting point for a national roadway system. With that point being Washington, D.C., the army truck train left on July 19, with 60 trucks and over 200 drivers and support personnel, complete with bridge and road-building equipment. The trucks made their way north from D.C. to Gettysburg, then turned west on the Lincoln Highway, driving through Bedford. The journey was completed in early September, with one officer writing, "The trip was difficult and tiring, but fun." That soldier was Lt. Col. Dwight D. Eisenhower.

In 1813, a wagon train under military escort carried DuPont powder from Wilmington, Delaware, to Erie, Pennsylvania, along a portion of the Lincoln Highway in Bedford.

In 1918, over 100 years after the first wagon train escort, an army truck transport carried munitions from Detroit to Philadelphia to be loaded on ships bound for France. General Pershing's supplies arrived via the Lincoln Highway and Bedford, Pennsylvania.

Motor vehicle traffic in the Bedford area was scarce well into the early 1900s. In 1905, only 13 cars were registered county-wide. The reasons for their lack of popularity included the mountainous terrain and lack of good roadways safe enough for motorized vehicles to travel.

For over 200 years, the intersection of Routes 30 and 31 has been the crossroad for countless travelers heading west through the mountains to Pittsburgh or south through the valley to Cumberland.

Built during the depression, the Pennsylvania Turnpike was the nation's first cross street and railroad-crossing-free interstate roadway. Its initial construction was a 160-mile link connecting Pittsburgh to Harrisburg. The idea for the highway was conceived after American engineers visited the Autobahn roadway system in pre-World War II Germany. Impressed with the German-engineered system of restricted access to a divided, cross-country highway without a speed limit, the decision was made to implement the same highway plan in the United States. Ground was broken, and the project commenced in October 1938, and was completed in October 1940. The turnpike consists of over 200 bridges and culverts and seven tunnels. Bedford, like many towns on the Route 30 corridor, saw automobiles pass by on the newer, faster highway.

Eight

A Grand Hotel

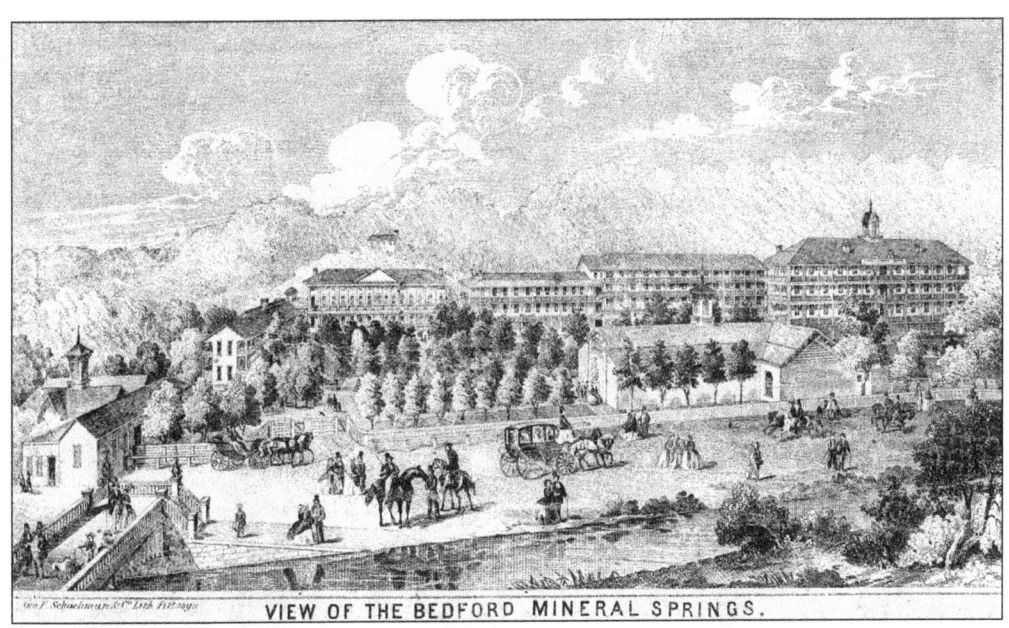

VIEW OF THE BEDFORD MINERAL SPRINGS.

The healing powers of the natural springs that flowed from the mountains around Bedford were known by the Native Americans who settled in the area over 7,000 years ago. It was not until the 19th century that one man realized not only the curative powers of these waters but also the commercial potential as well. Dr. John Anderson, born in 1770, was known as a man of intelligence and enterprise. He believed that the waters had great medicinal value. After studying medicine in Philadelphia, Anderson returned to practice in Bedford, traveling to his patients along the wooded trails and paths on horseback. He was a good doctor and a good businessman. It is a wonder if anyone predicted that one man's dream of a retreat to promote physical health and mental well-being could have endured for over 200 years.

In 1803, Dr. Anderson bought the original tract of land of 204 acres that contained a total of seven springs, which were the Mineral, Iron, Limestone, Sulfur, Sweet, Black, and Crystal Springs. Anderson then began the construction of many buildings, the first of which was a gentleman's bathhouse. By 1805, the word soon spread and people began to visit the area to enjoy the waters of these springs. By 1817, Anderson had acquired over 1,600 acres. The Bedford Springs Hotel had become the destination of many people in search of good health.

In this 1887 photograph, guests pose, with mineral water drinks in hand, for the camera. Many sport walking sticks, as it was common practice to stroll about the grounds of the hotel. Even in 1887, it was widely held that a brisk walk was good for the heart.

The springs themselves had individual gazebos constructed around them. The gazebos were of ornate construction, complete with benches, rocking chairs, and a supply of drinking glasses for the guests. Many even had hotel attendants.

In August 1855, the U.S. Supreme Court met at the hotel to argue the Passmore-Williamson Case. This was the only time in history the high court met of outside Washington, D.C.

Although the exact date of this photograph is unknown, a close examination of the flag shows that there are only 36 stars. This reveals that the picture was taken sometime prior to Nebraska being admitted into the Union. The star for the 37th state was officially added on July 4, 1867.

Because of its lavish amenities, beautiful surroundings, and secluded location, it is no wonder that the Bedford Springs Hotel was known as the Summer White House. For many years, the hotel played host to a great number of dignitaries, including Presidents Buchanan, Polk, Taylor, and Harrison, and future Pres. Ronald Reagan, Daniel Webster, and Aaron Burr. This photograph of the actual hotel registration book of August 1847 shows that then Secretary of State Buchanan was charged for his wife's and nurse's board. After his election, Buchanan became known as the bachelor president.

In over 100 years, the traveler's first view of the hotel, approaching from Bedford, has not changed. As you drive on Route 220 South, the heavily wooded roadway breaks into a clearing where the Bedford Springs Hotel stands exactly as it did at the beginning of the 20th century.

Less than 20 miles from the state of Maryland, the hotel served travelers from all over America. It is said that during the Civil War, officers from both the Union and the Confederacy dropped their families off at the hotel before going off to fight.

In 1890, the hotel was sold to two businessmen. Jesse Hilles of Baltimore, and Samuel Bancroft of Wilmington, Delaware, bought the complex for a reported $275,000. Both men made improvements that continued the tradition of the finest luxury and service.

The swimming pool, which still exists today, was the largest indoor pool of its kind when it was constructed.

In August 1858, the first transatlantic cable message was sent from the Queen of England to President Buchanan, who was staying at the hotel. The message read: "Come let us walk together. American genius and English enterprise have this day joined together the old and the new worlds. Let us hope that they may be as closely allied in bonds of peace, harmony, and kindred feeling." The message was signed, "Victoria, R."

By 1901, the hotel was under the direction of a new manager who set the goal of providing nothing but the best for the Bedford Springs guests. Particular attention was paid to the golf course and the landscaping, as the hotel hosted lawn concerts for its guests. By 1905, the hotel had been completely renovated. Dining and guest rooms were updated, and the kitchen was expanded to provide the finest foods for not only hotel guests but also the conventions that the ballroom facilities attracted.

COLONIAL BLDG. BEDFORD SPRINGS HOTEL. BEDFORD SPRINGS, PA

By the late 1890s, the hotel boasted nearly 2,000 acres, a large three-story brick building, a large four-story frame building, a three-story stone building, a three-story Swiss cottage, and a three-story frame building, all in use as a hotel with accommodations for 600 guests. The complex also included a brick kitchen, a laundry, a servants' quarters for a staff that topped over 200, stables for 50 horses, an ice house, a barn, a gardener's house, and two bottling factories.

One of the improvements made at the beginning of the 20th century was the addition of tennis courts and a bowling alley. The hotel now offered even more entertainment and activities for its guests, including horseback riding, croquet, and an 18-hole golf course.

By the beginning of the 20th century, the Bedford Springs Hotel was the region's largest employer, with over 200 staff members. In many cases, entire families worked at the hotel, including the children. Many of these children worked as flower and tobacco sellers, messengers, and entertainers.

The 1920s was a popular era at the hotel. Young guests and visitors sported coonskin coats and varsity sweaters as they enjoyed the opulent surroundings and fresh country air.

Added to the National Register of Historic Places in 1984, the hotel was designed and built by Solomon Filler and Donald Ross. The architectural design of all of the buildings include Greek Revival, Italianate, and Federal.

As this photograph shows, the hotel and its surrounding structures demonstrated the fine craftsmanship and pride of the local artisan. Most of the decorations that adorned the buildings and gazebos were hand-made on site. When available, local materials, such as hardwoods, were used for construction and furniture making, as an abundant supply of lumber was available. The management also called upon the local brick masons and stonemasons to erect the many needed wells, walls, and structures around the property.

As part of the ongoing activities offered by the hotel, professional tennis players and golf pros were employed by the Bedford Springs for the purpose of entertaining and instructing the guests. The staff also coordinated tournaments and exhibitions.

A group of guests stop to pose for a picture at the front gates of the hotel, in an era known as the Gay Nineties. Groups were common weekend visitors to the resort and traveled mostly by train.

On the hotel property, Red Oak Lake was created for the enjoyment of the guests. It offered swimming and water sports in the summer and ice-skating in the winter.

A writer from Philadelphia was passing through the area and made many observations about the Bedford Springs. He wrote, "No valley in Pennsylvania is fuller of historic tradition than that of which Bedford Springs is the gem. Every night the long saloon would resound with music and the laughter of dance."

Many prominent families spent time at the Bedford Springs, including those from Pittsburgh, Philadelphia, and Baltimore. One of these families was the Elkins from West Virginia. This photograph, taken in 1896, shows Slim Elkins with a towel and water bucket in hand.

Unlike many hotels and inns in the country, the Bedford Springs had its own band strictly for the entertainment of its guests. The musicians were not only employed to play at private celebrations, such as weddings and banquets, but would also travel the compound, entertaining in the gazebos. The Christmas holiday was an especially busy time for these talented musicians. They could be found by the hotel lobby fireside or accompanying carolers making their way around the guest accommodations.

Although the hotel offered a variety of pastime activities, one of the most popular was the impromptu card game. It was said that gamblers came from all over the region to try their luck. In the 1920s, many of the guests were the children of prominent families. The extravagances of these guests were a common sight, as the alcohol flowed freely and card games and drinking parties often lasted well into the night.

In the 1920s, plans were unveiled for an extensive expansion and remodeling project that involved the lobby and guest rooms. Just as construction was about to begin, the stock market crashed and America fell into a depression. The project was halted.

With the coming of the automobile came the need to care for these new horseless carriages. At the time of this photograph in 1908, the hotel employed a vehicle mechanic and caretaker.

Throughout the hotel's history, one standard was always constant. It was the pledge of the management and staff to always perform at their best in service to their guests. No detail was ever overlooked and no request was ever ignored because everyone believed that the customer always came first. Pictured here are the maids of 1902.

It was the duty of the maid supervisors, pictured here, to not only oversee the daily activities of the hotel's chambermaids, but also the facility's laundry services, employee scheduling, and guest services.

During World War II, the U.S. government utilized the hotel in two ways. The first was the establishment of a radio training school. Many of the hotel's facilities, such as the convention hall, were remodeled to accommodate over 7,000 navy personnel. The training facility remained open until early 1945. The other contribution made to the war effort was the housing of the nearly 200 Japanese diplomats and their families who were captured after Germany's collapse in Europe. These guests of the United States were exchanged for captured American POWs in Asia.

In 1803, a country doctor bought a few acres of land to establish a retreat that provided a place to heal, where one could enjoy the pristine beauty of the wilderness. Within a few years, this concept grew in popularity, as thousands of visitors came to a resort near Bedford now known as the Eden in the East. Through one civil and two world wars, the Bedford Springs Hotel provided a sanctuary for those seeking the healing powers of its mineral springs. By 1990, the hotel had seen its hey-day and closed its doors to guests. In the fall of 2005, new life, as invigorating as its healing waters, has been breathed into this grand lady, as plans for a renewal project have been announced. The grandeur of the Bedford Springs Hotel will be restored.

www.ingramcontent.com/pod-product-compliance
Lightning Source LLC
Chambersburg PA
CBHW080558110426
42813CB00006B/1338